Cernovcy

Botoşani

Suceava

Moldova

Bahlui

Iaşi

Prut

MOLDAVIA

Piatra-Neamţ

Vaslui

Bacău

HARGHITA

Miercurea-Ciuc

COVASNA

ania

Sfântu Gheorghe

Siret

Focşani

Braşov

P A T

Sinaia

Prahova

Galaţi

Brăila

Buzău

Tulcea

Danube Delta

Târgovişte

Ploieşti

Dâmboviţa

Slobozia

Ialomiţa

BLACK SEA

BUCHAREST

ACHIA

Călăraşi

Mamaia

Constanţa

Danube

Danube Canal - Black Sea

Costineşti

kandria

Giurgiu

Ruse

Mangalia

Bulgaria

CHIŞINĂU

Republic of Moldova

Ukraine

Official name:	Romania
Official language:	Romanian, Hu...
Area:	92,043 square...
Coastline:	140 miles
Climate:	Temperate continental
Population:	22,000,000
Capital:	Bucharest
Religions:	Christian Orthodox, Protestant, Roman Catholic
Currency:	1 Romanian leu = US $.33 = CAN $.33

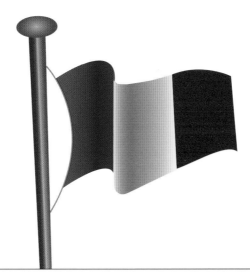

Looking at Europe

Romania

Jan Willem Bos

The Oliver Press, Inc.
Minneapolis

This edition published in 2011 by The Oliver Press, Inc.
Charlotte Square
5707 West 36th Street
Minneapolis, MN 55416-2510

Published by arrangement with KIT Publishers, The Netherlands
Copyright © 2008 KIT Publishers – Amsterdam

Library of Congress Cataloging-in-Publication Data

Bos, Jan-Willem.
  [Op bezoek in Roemenie. English]
  Romania / Jan Willem Bos.
        p. cm. -- (Looking at Europe)
  Includes index.
  ISBN 978-1-881508-86-1
  1. Romania--Juvenile literature.   I. Title.
  DR205.B66813 2010
  949.8--dc22

                                                    2009034604

Text: Jan Willem Bos
Photographs: Jan Willem Bos
Translation: Shannon Davidson
US editing: Anna Aman
Design and Layout: Miranda Zonneveld, Alkmaar, The Netherlands
Cover: Icon Productions, Minneapolis, USA
Cartography: Armand Haye, Amsterdam, The Netherlands

Picture Credits
Photographs: Jan Willem Bos
p. 3, and 16 (m) Andre Kom; p. 11 (b) Aad Littooij; p. 21 (t) Benjamin Gantikov;
p. 22 (t), 25 (t), 26 (t/m), 39 (t), 40 (t) Jo Goossens; p. 37 (m) Manfred Wirtz

ISBN 978-1-881508-86-1
Printed in The United States of America
14 13 12 11   5 4 3 2 1

Contents

Introduction

On January 1, 2007, Romania became a member of the European Union (EU). The country had already joined NATO on March 29, 2004. Their participation in the EU and NATO has given Romanians the feeling that they are no longer isolated and are part of the West.

From the end of World War II until 1989, Romania was dominated by the Soviet Union and was a communist country. There was only one political party, the Communist Party of Romania, and it had absolute control of everything. People were put in prison or thrown out of the country if they publicly did not agree with the party. In December 1989, the people of Romania revolted against the communist dictatorship and overthrew the powerful party leader, Nicolae Ceauşescu.

Free and democratic

Since Romania has become free and democratic, much has changed. Opinions can be voiced publicly, free elections are held, and state-owned companies have been replaced by private businesses.

Now that Romania has become a member of the EU, change and economic development will increase. This also means new challenges. Modernized farming methods, for example, will cause some people to lose their jobs. After a half-century under communist rule, the transition from communism to democracy and free markets will not be easy.

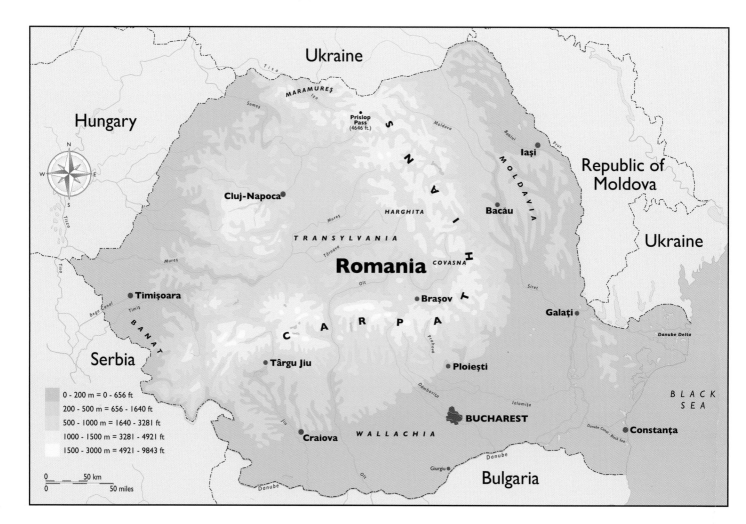

History

▲ *The Romanian coat of arms: an eagle with a cross in its mouth. The coat of arms also shows the different provinces of Romania.*

The current borders of Romania have only existed since 1945, when World War II ended. Before then, the country's long, turbulent history has featured many foreign invaders and frequently changing borders.

Romania has three historic regions: Wallachia, Moldavia, and Transylvania. The history of Transylvania, called *Siebenburgen* (seven fortresses) in German, is very different from that of the other two provinces.

Romania in the Middle Ages

Two thousand years ago, in present-day Romania, there was a huge empire called Dacia. It was ruled by Decabalus (king from 87 to 106). The Roman Emperor Trajan saw Dacia as a threat. Between 101 and 106, he organized two campaigns to conquer the empire. After the defeat of the Dacians and the death of Decabalus, the Dacian territory was occupied by subjects of the Roman Empire. They spoke Latin, the language from which Romanian was formed. One hundred and fifty years later, Emperor Aurelian, fearing the threatening, hostile barbarians on the northern borders, withdrew from Dacia. He relocated the Roman army and settlers to south of the Danube River, in what is now Serbia and Bulgaria.

◀ *The map of Dacia by Claudius Ptolemy (second century* BC*)*

Many nomadic tribes, such as the Huns and the Goths, moved through the region that is now Romania. Hungarians, or Magyars, came from Asia and settled northwest of the Carpathians, in the area called Transylvania. With few written documents, it is difficult to know exactly what happened in the period between the Roman withdrawal and the first Romanian principalities (territory ruled by a prince). The first Romanian principalities, Wallachia and Moldavia, were formed in the thirteenth and fourteenth centuries. It is said that a thousand years are missing from the history of Romania.

▶ *The medieval church of Densuş (thirteenth century)*

Dracula

The myth of the vampire Count Dracula of Transylvania, who sinks his teeth into the neck of his victims and drinks their blood, did not come from Romanian folklore. Rather, it came from the imagination of the Irish writer Bram Stoker, who in 1897 published his famous novel, *Dracula*. Stoker most likely was inspired by medieval vampire stories and paintings of Vlad Drăculea (1431-1476), who was famous for his cruelty. Vlad killed his enemies by impaling, or piercing, them on wooden stakes. He was given the nickname Vlad Țepeș, Vlad the Impaler. For the Romanians, Vlad was a national hero. He fought fiercely against the Turks, whose armies controlled Romanian territory. Dracula, however, is better known than Vlad. Films and cartoons continue to be produced about the character in Stoker's book. Francis Ford Coppola's famous film, *Bram Stoker's Dracula,* was made in 1992. Though *Dracula* was not originally a Romanian myth, Romania has plans to build an amusement park that is to be called Dracula Land.

▲ *A fifteenth-century portrait of Vlad Drăculea*

▶ *A letter, dated 1521, from the merchant Neacşu to the mayor of Kronstadt (now Braşov), is the oldest preserved document in the Romanian language. It is written in the Cyrillic (Slavonic) alphabet that the Romanians used until the nineteenth century.*

Ottoman rule

Wallachia and Moldavia were small provinces that quickly fell under the rule of their powerful neighbor to the south, the Ottoman Empire. To prevent having their territory occupied by the Ottoman Turks, Romania's princes sent both large sums of money and vast amounts of agricultural products to the Turkish sultan. For hundreds of years, the Romanians tried to prevent Turkish occupation. During the fifteenth century, the Moldavian monarch Ștephen the Great ruled for 48 years and fought dozens of battles against the Turks. In 1600, Michael the Brave of Wallachia (who ruled from 1593 to 1601) united, for the first time but briefly, the three provinces of Wallachia, Moldavia, and Transylvania. To this day, Romanians view him as one of the great heroes in their country's history.

◀ *This statue of Michael the Brave (Mihai Viteazul) stands in the center of Bucharest. It is customary to meet at the "horse's tail."*

◄ *The famous painting of "Revolutionary Romania" was painted by Constantin Daniel Rosenthal, a Jewish artist from Budapest, Hungary.*

The Phanariots (1711-1821)

At the beginning of the eighteenth century, another powerful neighboring country, Russia, took an interest in the Romanian provinces. To protect their power in Wallachia and Moldavia, the Turks appointed people they could trust to run the territories. These were high-ranking Greek officials who were in the service of the Turkish Sultan. Since they came from the Phanar section of Constantinople (now Istanbul), Turkey, they were called Phanariots. They ruled until 1821, when the Romanians, led by Tudor Vladimirescu, revolted against the Greek and Turkish oppressors. The uprising was quickly suppressed and Vladimirescu was killed. The Romanians did, however, gain something from the revolt, as Wallachia and Moldavia were governed once more by Romanian rulers.

National awareness

Transylvania had been part of the kingdom of Hungary since the eleventh century. In the seventeenth century, the Habsburg rulers of Austria brought both Transylvania and Hungary under their rule. Transylvania remained part of the Habsburg Empire until 1918. It was called the Austro-Hungarian Monarchy, or dual monarchy, from 1867 onwards. Half of the population in Transylvania was made up of Romanians. They had no political rights and their religion, the Christian-Orthodox faith, was not recognized. A Romanian nationalistic movement called the "Transylvanian School" came into being in the eighteenth century. The members of the movement protested that it was unfair that only Austrians and Hungarians had a say in important matters. They asked the Austrian Emperor for equal rights, but he would not grant them. This inspired more Romanians in Transylvania to become aware of their heritage and sympathize with the nationalist movement.

The Union of Wallachia and Moldavia (1859)

In the nineteenth century, the Romanians started to view the West, especially France, as a model for their own country. The people in the cities distanced themselves from their Eastern habits and clothing. Instead, they were inspired by the ideas of the French Revolution: "freedom, equality, and fraternity." In 1848, some groups tried to introduce a liberal constitution and social reforms. At the same time, they wanted to get rid of Turkish rule and Russia's influence. Though not successful, this movement gave rise to the idea that Romanians would be better off living in one country. In 1859, Colonel Alexandru Ioan Cuza was chosen as ruler of the United Principalities of Wallachia and Moldavia. Although this union was only meant to last while Cuza was on the throne, the two provinces stayed united and the name Romania was quickly adopted.

► *Alexandru Ioan Cuza (1820-1873), prince of the United Principalities of Wallachia and Moldavia*

Independence (1877)

Cuza turned out to be a corrupt ruler and was deposed in 1866. Carol von Hohenzollern-Sigmaringen, from the German royal family, was chosen to lead the united principalities. Romania was given a constitution for the first time. The Romanian constitution was based on the Belgian constitution, which was quite modern for those days. Under the leadership of King Carol I, who ruled for 48 years, advances in development and modernization were rapidly made. During the Russian-Turkish War of 1877-1878, Romania fought on the Russian side. The Romanians took this opportunity to declare their complete independence from Turkey. In Romania, this war is called the War of Independence.

The period of 1878 to 1914 brought Romania stability and progress. The majority of Romanians, however, were farmers who typically lived in great poverty. In 1907, the Peasant Revolt against large landowners broke out. It was violently suppressed, however, and thousands of peasants lost their lives.

► *King Carol I*

World War I (1914-1918) and Great Romania (1918-1940)

With the outbreak of World War I in 1914, Romania remained neutral. In 1916, however, the country joined forces with the Allies (France and England), who had promised Romania the province of Transylvania if the country fought with them against Germany and Austria-Hungary. On December 1, 1918, Transylvania declared independence from Austria-Hungary in favor of a union with Romania. December 1 is now a national day of celebration in Romania. Not everyone was pleased with this arrangement, however. The Hungarian residents of Transylvania wanted to remain with Hungary and fought, unsuccessfully, against the union. The country that came into being was Greater Romania. It was almost twice as big as the kingdom of Romania before 1914.

► *The Unity Square in Timişoara is named after the unification of the three Romanian monarchies.*

The Unknown Soldier

Just like in France after World War I, a monument was erected in Romania to "The Unknown Soldier," which represents one of the many soldiers who died during the war. In May 1923, ten coffins were dug up containing the bodies of unknown Romanian soldiers. A soldier was to be chosen from one of these. Amilcar C. Săndulescu, a war orphan, was asked which of the ten would receive the place of honor in the grave of the Unknown Soldier. He knelt in front of the fourth coffin and said, "This is my father." The coffin he had chosen was taken to Bucharest and buried with military honors.

▲ *Stamps issued for the occasion of the fiftieth anniversary of the unification of Transylvania with the rest of Romania*

The period between the two world wars brought industrialization to Romania and an increase in urban population. At the same time, the country suffered severly from the economic depression at the beginning of the 1930s. As in many other countries, an extreme nationalistic movement was born. One nationalistic group called the Iron Guard wanted only ethnic Romanians and not foreigners, Jews in particular, to have power within the country. They were not afraid to use violence to make their ideals and beliefs known. In 1938, King Carol II instituted a royal dictatorship and prohibited all political parties. This meant the end of the Romanian parliamentary democracy for the next fifty years.

▲ *A street scene in Bucharest during the inter-war period*

◀ *When this 100-leu bill was issued in 1947, Romania was not yet a people's republic. The design, however, already suggests communist images.*

World War II (1939-1945)

Once again, at the beginning of World War I, Romania was neutral. Despite this, the country was forced by Germany and the Soviet Union to give up large parts of its territory. A large piece of Transylvania (where many Hungarians lived) became part of Hungary. The northern and eastern part of Moldavia was annexed, or taken over, by the Soviet Union. King Carol II had to abdicate, or leave, his throne. His son, Mihai, replaced him. The actual power was in the hands of General Ion Antonescu, a military dictator. To win back the lost territories, Antonescu had Romania take part in the war on the side of Nazi Germany. On August 23, 1944, when Germany and its allies (including Romania) were losing the war, the young King Mihai arrested Antonescu. Romania then joined the Allied Forces. After the war, the country regained the part of Transylvania that had been given to Hungary. The east of Moldavia, however, stayed in the hands of the Soviet Union. When the Soviet Union collapsed in 1991, this area became an independent country called the Republic of Moldova.

The Communist Era (1947-1989)

At the end of World War II, Romania was occupied by the army of the Soviet Union, a communist state. Through unfair elections in 1946, the Communist Party rose to power, although very few in Romania believed in communism. The democratic parties were banned and their party leaders were thrown into prison. On December 30, 1947, King Mihai was forced to abdicate his throne. The People's Republic of Romania was proclaimed as the country's new name that very same day.

Now that the communists were in power, hundreds of thousands of opponents to the regime were imprisoned or deported, or forced to leave the country. The communist rulers also built many large factories, so many farmers went to the cities to work there, leaving the rural areas underdeveloped.

Palace of the Parliament

This building is also called the House of the People. Constructed in an old section of Bucharest, it is the largest building in Europe and the second largest in the world after the Pentagon. A road that is 492 feet wide leads up to the House, which was supposed to be named the Boulevard of the Victory of Socialism. It is said that only Romanian materials were used in its construction, including 2,800 chandeliers, 236,800 square feet of carpet, 3,445 tons of crystal, 37,674 square feet of leather, 35 million square feet of marble, and many tons of wood. The construction cost about $6 billion. When the December Revolution took place in 1989, the Palace was nearly completed. The first man to greet a wildly enthusiastic crowd from the central balcony was not the dictator Nicolae Ceaușescu, however, but singer Michael Jackson. After the fall of communism, the new government changed the name to the Palace of the Parliament.

In the 1960s, the leaders of Romania became slightly more relaxed. Relations with the West improved slightly. In 1965, Nicolae Ceaușescu became the leader of the Communist Party and, therefore, the most powerful man in the country. He began as more of an independent leader, so for the most part he came to be viewed favorably in both the West and also in Romania. During the years that followed, however, he became a ruthless dictator. He pursued a disastrous economic policy and oppressed the population with the help of the Securitate, the feared secret police. While Ceaușescu was building an immense palace in Bucharest, many Romanians suffered great hardships. This era is called the era of the three "f's": *foame, frică, frig* (hunger, fear, cold). At the same time, Ceaușescu let himself be praised as "the genius of the Carpathians" and "the most loved son of the people." A large number of television programs were about the "great deeds" of his wife, Elena, and himself.

Investim în oameni.

Revolution and transition (1989-present day)

In 1989, communist regimes were overthrown in various countries of the "Eastern Bloc" (as the communist states were called then). The people revolted against oppression and poverty. The revolt was non-violent almost everywhere except in Romania. In December 1989, a successful, but violent, uprising against Ceauşescu and communism took place. About a thousand people died, among them many school pupils and students who had bravely protested against the dictatorship. Ceauşescu and his wife were executed on Christmas Day 1989 by a firing squad.

Romania was a free country now that the communists were removed from power. There was no longer any censorship. Political parties could be set up again and free elections held. A few years after the revolution, all political parties agreed to do their best so that Romania could become a member of NATO and the European Union.

The years after the fall of communism were not easy. Many people found the transition from communism to a free society to be chaotic. They were also disappointed at how slowly reforms were made. While some businessmen became very wealthy, the unemployed, elderly, and handicapped remained very poor. Some people longed for communism again, since life seemed simpler and easier then.

In the years between the fall of communism and the entry into the European Union, much changed in Romania. The country is no longer a dictatorship with a state-led economy. Romania is a parliamentary democracy now with a free-market economy of privately owned businesses. There is political and economic freedom and Romanians can travel throughout all of Europe without a visa. However, not all the problems of half a century of communism have been solved.

Romania seems to be taking steps towards a better future by becoming a member of NATO (since 2004) and the EU (since January 1, 2007). There is certainly more development. Most importantly, the freedom of the people is now guaranteed. The fact that they are part of the West is very important to the Romanians, especially since Romanians believe that Romania shares a history with western European countries.

▶ *There is freedom of the press in Romania after the fall of communism. But now, there are so many reading options, it's hard to know what to choose!*

▲ *Conditions are often poor in the Romanian countryside.*

Country

Romania (in Romanian: *România,* with an emphasis on the "i") lies in the center of Europe. It borders Hungary in the northwest (278 miles), Ukraine in the north and east (431 miles), the Republic of Moldova in the northeast (423 miles), Bulgaria in the south (392 miles), and Serbia in the southwest (339 miles).

The Black Sea coast in the east is 120 miles long. The Danube river forms the southern border with Serbia and Bulgaria. It is 466 miles long. The distance between London and Bucharest is about 1,300 miles, about three and a half hours by plane. It is about 4,150 miles from Bucharest to New York City.

Cities and rural areas

Romania is a medium-sized country, but the largest in southeastern Europe. It has an area of 92,043 square miles, slightly smaller than the state of Oregon. Romania's population is approximately 22 million, which makes it among the ten most-populous countries in Europe.

About 2 million people live in the capital, Bucharest. This is roughly 10 percent of the country's population. If temporary residents are also counted, the percentage would be higher, since the city attracts many workers from other areas. Although many factories were built in the cities during the communist era, and many people migrated to the cities then, about half of the Romanian population still lives in rural areas. They live in one of about 13,000 villages spread across the country.

While many old structures have been destroyed for blocks of apartment buildings in the cities, most villages still have traditional housing. The comforts of modern plumbing are not always found in the countryside, where much of the population ekes out a living from vegetable gardens and a few cows and sheep. This way of life may look charming and appealing at first, but there is still a lot of hardship and poverty in rural Romania.

▶ *"This is where I live!"*

This is my darling....The only problem is, he can't cook!

Man with foal – In autumn, Ion goes to the woods with his horse and cart to gather firewood. The wood-burning stove is not only for keeping the house warm, but also for cooking. Large animals such as horses play a very important role in the daily lives of many villagers across Romania's countryside, although they hope to have enough money one day to buy a tractor or truck instead.

Climate

Romania has a temperate continental climate, which means the four seasons are clearly defined. In the recent years, however, spring has been so warm that it appears as if winter just moves into summer, skipping spring entirely. The average temperature in the winter is 27°F. In the summer, the average temperature is 75°F. In various parts of the country, there are noticeable differences in the weather. The eastern province of Moldavia is affected by the extreme Russian climate. Winters are colder and the summers are hotter there. However, in the Banat, the far west of the country, the climate is affected favorably by the Mediterranean.

▼ *Winter in Sibiu, with the Carpathians in the background*

Weather changes

In the past ten years, Romania has had extreme weather conditions. For example, there has been regular flooding because of prolonged rainfall. In 2005, the rivers rose over their banks six times due to the constant downpours. Tens of thousands of people lost their houses. These structures, made of mud and straw, could not withstand the water. On the other hand, summers have often been very hot and dry in the past few years. In 2004, the rainfall held off for so long that the water level in the Danube River was at an all-time low. For the first time in living memory, people could wade through to Bulgaria on the other side of the river. The summer of 2007 was also miserable for those who could not leave the cities. There was one heatwave after another, with temperatures reaching almost 104°F. In the summer of 2010, severe flooding in the northeast of the country took more than 20 lives, mostly from drowning.

Transhumance

Moving livestock in a seasonal cycle used to be a common sight in all mountainous areas of Europe. Today, Romania is one of the few countries where this still takes place. The moving of sheep in Romanian is *transhumanţă*. In English-speaking countries, the word *transhumance* is used. At the beginning of autumn, shepherds gather on the high mountain slopes of the Carpathians. With their flocks, they set off for the Danube plains. There they will spend their winter months. Around Easter time, when the snow has melted, they go back to higher regions. Lambs are then slaughtered for the Easter meal. In times past, flocks of sheep traveled many miles and numbered a thousand or more animals. There are folklore traditions in Romania linked to transhumance, such as "measuring the milk." This was done to find out how much cheese the owners of the sheep were entitled to.

Provinces and districts

Romania is divided into forty districts (*judeţe*), plus the capital Bucharest. Such a large number of districts is rather difficult for the government to coordinate, so eight economic development regions have been formed. Within a region, local authorities work together on public projects. In addition, there are a number of historical provinces that have only just become part of Romania. Between the Carpathian Mountains and the Danube lies Wallachia, called *Ţara Românească* in Romanian history. It literally means the "Romanian country." To the east of the mountains lies Moldavia (*Moldova*). The eastern part of historic Moldavia, called Bessarabia, has often been annexed by Russia or the Soviet Union during its history. Since 1991, it has been the independent Republic of Moldova. Transylvania (*Transilvania* or *Ardeal* in Romanian) lies to the north and west of the Carpathians.

Rivers and the sea

The Danube (*Dunărea* in Romanian) is the second longest river in Europe (after the Volga). It rises in the Black Forest of southwestern Germany, then flows through central Europe to form Romania's southern border with Bulgaria.

From the forests of the Carpathians, rivers such as the Jiu, the Olt, and the Prahova wind their way downward. They travel through the mountains until they flow into the Danube.

The Danube splits into three smaller rivers at the town of Tulcea before flowing into the Black Sea. The Black Sea coast has broad beaches. Many seaside resorts can be found on these beaches. The most famous is Mamaia, just north of the town of Constanţa.

▼ *The Danube makes its way towards the Black Sea through the gap in the Carpathians called the Iron Gate Gorge.*

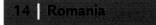

◀ *Houses in the valley of the Sebeş*

Flag

The Romanian flag has three vertical stripes: blue, yellow, and red. During the communist years, the state's coat of arms was placed in the middle yellow bar. This was torn out during the revolution. A new coat of arms had been designed, but it is no longer part of the flag.

Money

Romanian money is called the *leu*, the plural of which is *lei*, and is divided into 100 *bani*. Leu means "lion." It probably came from the Dutch "lion thaler," which was a coin that was in use in Romania during the seventeenth and eighteenth centuries. The word "dollar" also comes from the Dutch thaler, which was pronounced *daler* in Dutch and Low German. The English adopted this form and eventually changed the spelling to dollar. New Romanian bank notes have been designed to a size similar to that of the European common currency, the euro. The country is planning to switch its currency to the euro in 2012-2014. To make counterfeiting more difficult, Romanian bank notes are no longer made of paper, but of polymer, a kind of plastic.

▲ *On the five-leu bill is the portrait of the composer George Enescu (1881-1955).*

National Anthem

Since the revolution of 1989, Romania has had a new national anthem, called "Awaken thee, Romanian!" The song was written during the revolution of 1848 by Andrei Muresanu. Singing (or even humming) the song was forbidden during the communist era because it encourages revolt against tyrants. Communists replaced the song with one of their own, called "Three Colors." During the widespread uprising of 1989, protesters in the streets sang the song again and it became the new national anthem chosen by the people. Romanians celebrate July 29 as National Anthem Day. Here is the first of the song's eleven stanzas:

> *Awaken thee, Romanian, awake from deadly slumber*
> *Forced upon you by barbaric tyrants*
> *Now or never, fashion a new Fate,*
> *That shall put to shame your enemies.*

◀ *Cat guards laundry*

Cities and towns

Slightly more than half of the population of Romania lives in the cities. Many cities have drab apartment blocks that were built during the communist era. However, there are still many beautiful things to admire in the cities, such as castles, old churches, and picturesque neighborhoods.

▲ It is nicer in the country at Grandma and Grandpa's than it is in the city.

▲ The fountains in the center of Bucharest are lovely and cool in the summer.

On the north side of the city there are little lakes surrounded by parks. The most famous one is the Cişmigiu Garden, dating from the nineteenth century. It is a beautifully structured park with many ponds, statues, and outdoor cafes. This park forms a haven of peace in the busy city center.

Bucharest

About two million people live in the capital, Bucharest (in Romanian: *Bucureşti*). According to legend, the city owes its name to a shepherd named Bucur who was its founder. It is more likely, however, that the city was founded by merchants in the fourteenth century. In 1659, Bucharest became the capital of Wallachia. In 1862, it became the capital of Romania. Bucharest was given the nickname "Little Paris" or "Paris of the East" before World War II. It was nicknamed this because many buildings in the city were built by French architects and also because, like Paris, it had a flourishing cultural and artistic life.

Bucharest is situated on the river Dâmboviţa, which has been directed into channels in the city and even disappears underground in the city center.

▼ In the Cişmigiu Gardens in Bucharest there is a special corner for chess players. One can always find an opponent to play here.

Roller Skating – Bucharest is known as a city full of parks. It's even nicknamed the "Garden City." The largest park is Herestrău, just north of the city center. It has a large lake on which you can go boating. Nearby is the Village Museum, an outdoor museum with houses, windmills, village schools, and wooden churches. You can spend a couple of lazy hours in an outdoor cafe, or you can be more active and jog, walk, or roller skate. There is room for everyone. The park was opened in 1936.

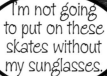

▲ *"The street where I chased after Ana"*

The center of Bucharest is largely taken up by the Palace of the Parliament and newly built houses around it. In the 1980s, a large part of the old town was demolished to make room for the immense palace. This was done on the orders of the communist leader Nicolae Ceauşescu. There are only a few streets of the old town center left. Since 2007, after years of neglect, these streets are being restored.

▲ *Renovation in the old center of Bucharest*

Bucharest is situated in an earthquake zone. In the earthquakes of 1940 and 1977, part of the center was destroyed. The earthquake of 1977 measured a powerful 7.2 on the Richter scale. More than 1,500 people were killed and more than 30,000 buildings were destroyed. Much of the debris from the 1977 earthquake was cleared to make way for the Palace of the Parliament

Bucharest is the political, cultural, and economic center of the country. Because of this, it is a very busy city. New buildings are being built in the center, as well as in the suburbs. At the same time, Bucharest is an interesting and dynamic city that attracts many Romanians from across the country. Not only are most of the top jobs found here, it is also the center for entertainment

of all kinds. When people in the provinces are fast asleep, Bucharest is still bubbling with activity.

While no other city in Romania comes close to matching the size and importance of Bucharest, the country has many smaller cities that have much to offer in their own right.

▶ *Musicians in the Bucharest subway*

Iaşi

Iaşi, the country's second largest city, has about 400,000 inhabitants. The name used to be spelled "Jassy" worldwide. Iaşi lies on the river Bahlui and is called "the town of the seven hills," just like Rome and Istanbul. In historic documents, Iaşi is mentioned for the first time in 1408. There are buildings older than this in the city, however, so we know Iaşi existed long before this. In 1640, the first school to teach Romanian was established. Iaşi was the capital of Moldavia from 1566 to 1862. After the unification of Wallachia and Moldavia in 1862, Bucharest became the only capital of Romania. At the end of the nineteenth century, Iaşi was modernized. It was decorated with beautiful buildings such as the Palace of Culture, the National Theater "Vasile Alecsandri" (a poet who lived from around 1821 to 1890), and the Alexandru Ioan Cuza University.

▶ *A dog to guard the sheep some day?*

Cluj-Napoca

Cluj is the historic capital of the province of Transylvania. The town is also known by the Hungarian name, Kolozsvár, and the German name, Klausenburg. Since 1974, the city has been called Cluj-Napoca. The old Latin name of the city has been added to emphasize the fact that Romans lived in the area 2,000 years ago. Up to World War I, the whole of Transylvania, and therefore Cluj, belonged to Austria-Hungary. Most of the inhabitants were Hungarian. Now only about 20 percent are Hungarian. There is a Hungarian opera and a Hungarian theater. Romanian, Hungarian, German and, more recently, English are all taught at the famous Babeş-Bolyai University. This is the largest university in the country.

From 1992 to 2004, Cluj had a mayor, Gheorghe Funar, with so much Romanian pride that he had all the benches in the city painted in the colors of the Romanian flag. He did this to emphasize the Romanian character of this multicultural city.

◄ *There are trolleybuses in many Romanian cities. This one has an advertisement for a shopping mall.*

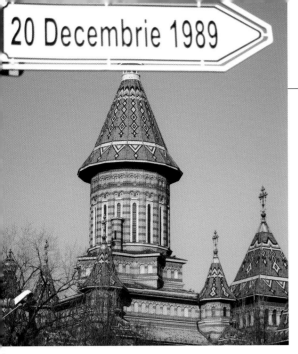

20 Decembrie 1989

The city of the revolution – Timişoara is the city where, on December 16, 1989, the revolution started that ended communism. It began when authorities forcefully wanted to transfer the Hungarian clergyman, László Tökes, to another town. When they attempted this, protests broke out. In the following days, the protests grew into a major uprising against the dictatorship. Fearing the rebellion would grow even stronger, government security forces and the army fired at the demonstrators, killing many, especially young people. Only four days after the revolution started, on December 20, Timişoara declared itself to be the first non-communist city in Romania. The revolution in Bucharest had yet to begin. In total, 1,100 died during the Romanian revolution of 1989.

▲ On December 22, 1989, communism was overthrown. In the background is the Romanian Orthodox cathedral of Timişoara.

▲ This bookseller in Timişoara also sells postcards and calendars.

Timişoara

Timişoara is the multicultural capital of the western region called Banat. The city gets its name from the river Timiş that flows through the city. The Bega Canal, which is partly in Romania and partly in Serbia, also flows through Timişoara. The canal was dug in the eighteenth century. Particles of mud and clay, called silt, are deposited by flowing water. Since the eighteenth century, this silt has built up in the canal. Since 1956, the canal has no longer been usable because of the silt. There are plans, however, to dig out the canal again. In 1855, Timişoara was the first city in the Habsburg Empire to have electricity. In 1884, it was the first city in Europe to have streetlights. Timişoara had a brewery as early as 1718. This city is lovely and cultural, with 14,500 historic monuments, more than any other Romanian town or city. Romanians, Hungarians, Germans, and Serbs all live together in Timişoara. It is the only European city with three National Theaters: one Romanian, one Hungarian, and one German. The Romanians remain the majority in the population, however.

Timişoara has experienced strong economic growth since the 1990s. This is especially due to foreign investors who have built businesses and factories there. Timişoara is also a center of education. Young people from all parts of Romania, but also an increasing number of young people from the EU countries, go to Timişoara to study. There are many places for young people to go and share ideas with their peers, or just to have fun. Timişoara has a famous jazz cafe, for example. Other outdoor cafes are also open from April onward.

◄ A game of soccer in Timişoara

Constanţa

The city of Constanţa lies on the Black Sea. This coastal town is not only the most important port of Romania, it is also the most important arrival and departure point for tourists who have come to enjoy the sunny beaches and resorts along the Black Sea. It is the fourth largest port in Europe, just after Rotterdam, Antwerp, and Marseille. Where the city now lies, there once was a Greek colony called Tomis. The Roman Emperor Augustus deported the Greek poet Ovid to this city of Tomis. Ovid did not like being away from his homeland at all. He sent poems back home that were filled with sorrow and he pleaded to be allowed back. A statue of Ovid is now in the central square of Constanţa. In this same central square, the Archaeological Museum and a beautifully preserved mosaic can also be found. Constanţa has the largest mosque in Romania, built between 1910 and 1912. It was the first building to be built with reinforced concrete, meaning it was built both with concrete and steel bars for more strength. The area between the Danube River and the Black Sea, where Constanţa is situated, has only belonged to Romania since 1878. Before that, it was part of the Ottoman Empire. There still are minorities of Turks and Tartars (an ethnic group that speaks Turkish) living in the city.

Other cities

Craiova is the capital of the southern region of Oltenia. It is an industrial center where, among other things, cars, engines, and equipment are made. **Piteşti** is a slightly smaller city, with 190,000 inhabitants, in south-central Romania. Since 1966, a factory there has made cars with the brand name Dacia. The company is now owned by Renault. Piteşti, also called the "city of tulips," holds a Tulip Festival every year. The tulip was originally a Turkish flower. The Romanian word for tulip, *lalea*, is derived from the Turkish word, *lále*.

▼ *The Constanţa casino in winter. This casino hosted a royal gala for the 1914 visit of the Russian Imperial Family to Romania.*

Braşov, in central Romania, has 320,000 inhabitants. Originally a German city with the name Kronstadt, Braşov is an important industrial town with tractor and truck factories. It is also a popular place to enjoy winter sports. The ski resort Poiana Braşov is only seven miles outside of Braşov. The Black Church, dating from the fourteenth century, is the city's most famous building. The church got its name in 1689 when a fire burnt it completely black.

Ploieşti, just north of Bucharest, has 135,000 inhabitants. It is the center of the Romanian petroleum industry.

Sibiu has 160,000 residents. Sibiu is a flourishing cultural and economic center in the south of Transylvania. The peaks of the Carpathians are visible from this city. Sibiu was founded in the twelfth century by Germans who gave it the name Hermannstadt. Sibiu was the capital of Transylvania in the eighteenth and nineteenth centuries. The palace of Baron Samuel Brukenthal was built here between 1778 and 1788. In his will, the Baron wished for his palace to become a museum upon his death. It became the first museum in Romania. Before World War II, the majority of the population was German. Now, there are less than 6,000 people of German heritage left. In 2007, Sibiu was the first Romanian city, together with the western European city of Luxemburg, to be named a European Capital of Culture.

► *The village of Cristian (in the district of Sibiu) has a fortified church. The villagers could once seek shelter here.*

◄ *Sheep graze in Maramureş, a rural region in the north.*

▲ *Try keeping your shoes mud-free walking on this road....*

Transportation

The Romanian road system is poorly developed. There are hardly any freeways or highways. This means that traffic has to go through towns and villages.

As traffic increases, many drivers of both cars and trucks face a number of issues. They have to drive in dangerous situations, such as having many pedestrians and animals near or on the road. Romanian drivers also have a notorious reputation. Their reckless driving causes many accidents on two-lane roads.

New freeways

Before the fall of communism, Romania had only 62 miles of freeways. Even then, it was only between Bucharest and Piteşti. Since then, the "Sun's Freeway" from Bucharest to the Black Sea has been partially built. The "Autostrada Transylvania" is another freeway being built. This goes from the Hungarian border to the city of Braşov where, in the future, it will be linked to the new A1 leading to Bucharest. Networks of roads within the provinces are also being repaired. Ring roads, or roads that bypass a town, are also being built around Bucharest to help the flow of traffic. There is even more work to be done in the villages. Only the main road through a village is made of asphalt, while the other streets are simply dirt roads. This means that when it rains in rural Romania, the roads turn into mud and make it even more unpleasant to travel through.

Even though people are working hard to make the roads better, the improvements can barely keep up with the growth of traffic. Since the revolution of 1989, car ownership has risen by 10 percent each year. The result of this is that many cities develop a serious traffic problem. The traffic in Bucharest at times can come to a complete halt. It is sometimes quicker to walk. For pedestrians, it is quite a challenge to weave in and out of parked cars. Romaninan cities have an issue with parking. There are not a lot of parking spaces, so many drivers just park their cars on the pavement.

▶ *In Bucharest, one driver has chosen to solve his parking problem by parking right on the sidewalk.*

"A little cycling and I'll just make it there on time."

Since 1979, Bucharest has had a subway, which continues to grow in popularity. For those who want to travel above ground, there are buses, trams, and trolleybuses. There are not many people who ride bikes in the city. However, in the country, bikes are used often.

▲ *This ticket is good for one ride on the bus, trolleybus, or tram.*

▲ *In many Romanian cities there are trolleybuses.*

In the country, horses and carts are often used, both to transport people and goods. It is estimated that there are 750,000 horse-drawn carts still in use. They share the roads with motor vehicles. However, it is dangerous for them to travel at night

because they do not have lights to warn other drivers that they are also on the road. Sadly, many accidents happen after sunset. Not very many people have a car in the country, and public transportation is not developed enough to reach these areas.

Children have to walk far to get to school. Not all villages have schools for secondary education. So, if they want to continue their education after primary school, the students have to live at a boarding school or with a family in the city.

◄ *Environmentally friendly and no road tax to pay, but also dangerous after sunset*

▶ *Ferry across the Danube. The ferry doesn't have a motor, so it is pushed by a tug boat.*

Shipping

The Danube is the only river that is deep enough and wide enough for large boats. Most ships and other vessels on their way to the Black Sea avoid the Danube delta, or the mouth of the river with deposits of soil. Instead, they use the canal called the Danube-Black Sea Canal. The digging for this canal started in the 1950s. Most of the work at that time was carried out by forced labor. Those forced to do the labor were people who did not agree with the communist regime. Work stopped in 1955, but was started again in 1975. The work was finished in 1984, and cost around one and a half billion dollars. However, the canal itself only brings in about one and a half million dollars a year.

▲ *From the station in Piteşti, the "Blue Arrow" is ready for the journey to Bucharest.*

The port of Constanţa is one of the largest ports in Europe. It is a major transit port between both central and eastern Europe on one side, and central Asia and the Middle East on the other. A port has existed here for more than 2,500 years. The first stone of the current port was laid in 1896 by King Carol I. Since then, the port has constantly been modernized and expanded. The lastest modernizations are a 2004 container terminal, where cargo can be stored, and a passenger terminal in 2005.

Railways

The Romanian Rail Company (*Căile Ferate Române*, CFR) has an extensive network of railway lines with a total of 9,000 miles. Ten percent of the railway company is owned by private firms. CFR has been modernizing the railway since 2000. New locomotives and carriages have been bought and many stations have been remodeled. Since Romania is a large country and takes quite some time to cross, there are many sleeping cars. If you take the sleeper train at eleven at night from Bucureşti-Nord (Bucharest-North) to Iaşi, you will be completely rested when you arrive at 5:40 the following morning. The longest train journey in Romania, from Suceava in the northeast to Timişoara in the west, takes 15 hours.

Aviation

Although fifteen Romanian cities have airports, flights within the country are not a common mode of transportation. Transportation by car, train, or bus is still more popular, especially since plane tickets are so expensive. The most important international airport is Henri Coandă, to the north of Bucharest in the village of Otopeni. Timişoara, Cluj, Constanţa, and Sibiu also have international airports. The airport in Bucharest before the wars, Băneasa, is used now only by charter planes and private aircraft.

The national airline company, TAROM (*Transporturile Aeriene Române*, Romanian Air Transport), flies to a great many destinations in Europe and the Middle East. British Airways, for example, now flies ten times a week from Bucharest to London and back.

◀ *TAROM flies throughout Europe.*

People and culture

Throughout its history, many different peoples have lived on Romanian soil. Today, Romania also has various national minorities. Ethnic Romanian people are still the majority of the population, however.

▲ *You can always try your luck and buy a lottery ticket.*

Population groups

In 2002, a census was carried out in which people could indicate which population group they belonged to. It was discovered that 90 percent of the population in Romania is Romanian, although some feel that they are really Moldavians. There is also an important Romanian minority in North Bukovina, an area that now belongs to Ukraine. In addition, there are significant Romanian minorities in Serbia and Hungary. The next planned census is in 2011.

The largest minority group in Romania, with 1.4 million people, is the Hungarians (also called Magyars). This makes up almost seven percent of the country's population. Relations between Romanians and Hungarians have often been tense, but have also improved over time. Hungarian is actually considered an official language in a city if at least 20 percent of the population there speak it.

▲ *The daily paper* Libertatea *is popular throughout Romania.*

The Hungarians celebrate their national day on March 15. They continue this traditional celebration in Romania as well. With pride, the members of the Hungarian minority put out their flag, Hungary's three horizontal stripes of red, white, and green. They also put on their national costume and hold processions and parades.

◀ *Not everyone has a mobile phone, so public phones are provided in the cities.*

▶ *A Roma family has just collected wood in the forest.*

The Roma, as the gypsies prefer to be called, are the third largest population group. The Roma in Romania form between two and three percent of the population. In the census, many said that they felt Romanian or Hungarian. This depended on which language they were brought up with or most comfortable speaking.

Many Roma live in severe poverty. They live in huts in the country they built themselves or in run-down buildings in neglected neighborhoods. It is unfortunate, but not surprising then, that the life expectancy of Roma is 15 years less than that of other population groups. The government has various programs to improve life for the Roma, but it is a difficult task.

◀ *Some Roma travel in covered wagons for part of the year.*

The Roma keep to their own traditions and customs, and reject the culture of the *gadjes* (the non-Roma). There is sadly also a lot of prejudice against the Roma, and it is difficult for them to find work. Some Roma are successful because gypsy music is very popular, not just in Romania but abroad as well. They earn some money by performing their music and selling their CDs. The band Taraf de Haidouks ("band of gypsies") is very popular.

There used to be many Germans in Romania, especially in Transylvania. The Germans in the center of Transylvania settled there in the twelfth century. They are called Saxons, even though they did not come from Saxony. They actually came from the south of the Netherlands. Near the town of Alba Iulia there is a village called Bărăbanţ. This is derived from Brabant, a southern Dutch province. Germans also settled in the western region of Banat in the eighteenth century. They are called Schwaben. In 1930, there were still 800,000 ethnically German people living in Romania. However, due to mass emigration, there are now only about 60,000 left.

◀ *Billboards hanging on the sides of buildings may obstruct the view for those within, but they do bring in money for businesses.*

► *A house in Şieu with Christ on the cross*

Other minorities include the Turks and the Tartars (55,000). They live mainly in the area between the Danube and the Black Sea. Before World War II, there were also many Jews in Romania. Because they were persecuted and massacred during the war, many emigrated to Israel and the United States. Their numbers have dropped to less than 6,000 now.

Religion

Romanians are very religious. During the last census 20,000, or only 0.1 percent, said they did not believe in God. Almost all Romanians belong to the Romanian-Orthodox Church. Since they are Christian-Orthodox believers, they have the same religion as, for example, the Greeks, the Bulgarians, and the Russians. The Romanians view their religion as an essential part of their national identity. They are the only people with a foundation in the Roman Empire who are not Roman Catholic, but Christian Orthodox.

The Hungarians and Germans in Romania are usually Catholic or Protestant (Reformed). There are also Romanians who belong to new Protestant churches such as the Adventist church or the Pentecostal church.

◄ *In "the merry cemetery" in Săpânţa (in the district of Maramureş), the crosses are decorated and have rhymes.*

Name day

Most Romanians have at least one first name that is derived from the name of a saint. The name day of that saint is celebrated as the person's birthday. On December 6, the day of Saint Nicolas (in Romanian: *Sfântul-Nicolae*), everyone with the name Niculae or Nicolae and also Nicole and Nicoletta celebrate their birthdays. On January 7, the name day of Sfântul-Ioan (Saint John or John the Baptist), almost 2 million Romanians with the names of Ion, Ioan, Iona, Ionel, or Ionuţ have their day of celebration. Sometimes name days are an even bigger celebration than a person's actual birthday. It is common to receive flowers, chocolate, and cards on your name day.

(speech bubble) Can we add another one ?

The communist regime was officially atheist. In other words, it did not believe in religion. The people, however, were not necessarily forbidden to go to church. Since the fall of communism in 1989, a revival of religion has occured. The churches are full of people on important religious holidays. Many young people also choose to live as monks or nuns in one of the many monasteries or convents in Romania. On October 14, Saint Paraschiva's Day, at least one million Romanians make a pilgrimage to the town of Iaşi. The relics of the saint have been kept here since 1641.

Posting

Posters have been pasted up everywhere in the center of Bucharest. An advertisement for an intensive yoga course claims to change people and give them insight. It also covers up other posters beneath it, including an announcement for a concert by the band Deep Purple.

Declining Population

Romanian families are usually small. Many Romanians went abroad to find a better life after the fall of communism. The Romanian population is rapidly decreasing due to both this emigration and lower birthrates.

In 2000, there were 22.3 million Romanians. In 2007, there were only 21.5 million. It is expected that there will only be 16.8 million left in 2050. A lot of people, not only those in Romania, think that the aging population is going to be a problem in fifty years. Many elderly people will then be dependent upon the younger generation. The potential problem is that this younger generation will likely have fewer people to support them. Perhaps it will turn out better than expected. Older people may continue working longer and young people will then be able to find jobs that involve caring for the elderly.

▶ *Bianca is helping her grandfather pick apples.*

◄ *"I help my parents on the weekend at the market. I earn a little pocket money, too."*

Romanians believe family life is very important. It is customary for the elderly to live with their children, even after they are married and have families of their own. They can look after the grandchildren, especially since, in most families, both the mother and the father work. Childcare in Romania outside the home is not very common.

When Romanians entered the EU on January 1, 2007, there were about 1.5 million Romanians who worked abroad (see page 42). Most of them see their foreign stay as temporary. Many, however, will most likely not return home because they have settled into their new country. They have their work and children who go to school and have friends there.

▶ *Mihai Eminescu*

Romanian language

A Romanian poet named Mihai Eminescu claimed that because the Romanian language sounded so beautiful, it was proof that Romanians themselves were elevated and sophisticated people. Romanians spoke Old Church Slavonic (or Old Bulgarian) as an official language in church and government until the sixteenth century. A letter from 1521 is the oldest remaining document in the Romanian language (see page 6).

This is a fascinating book.

Bookworms
Romanians are great book lovers. Secondhand books are eagerly snatched up. There are not many Romanian writers who are known abroad, but Romanians are proud of their national poet Mihai Eminescu (1850-1889).

Some words in Romanian

Da	Yes
Nu	No
Bună ziua!	Good day!
Bună seara!	Good evening!
Salut!	Hello!
Ce mai faci?	How are you?
Bine	Fine
Noroc!	Cheers! / Happiness!
Mulţumesc	Thank you
La revedere!	Good bye!
Unu, doi, trei...	One, two, three...
Bucureştiul este capitala României	Bucharest is the capital of Romania

Romanian is directly descended from Latin, just like French, Spanish, and Italian. However, Romanian is different in many ways from these other Romance languages of the West. Romanian contains many words from other languages, such as Greek, Turkish, German, and Hungarian. From the nineteenth century onward, when the heritage of a language rooted in Latin became popular, more French words were adopted. The Romanians used the Cyrillic (Slavonic) alphabet, with a few exceptions, up to the nineteenth century. Then they decided to write Romanian in the Latin alphabet. In Romanian, one character is used for each sound. Romanian also has the letters ş, ţ, ă, â and î, pronounced "sj," "ts," silent "e," and the last two sound like "uh."

Sports

As soon as the weather is nice, these boys play soccer outside of their village, Odvoş. Soccer is the most popular sport in Romania and the country has produced many famous soccer players, such as Gheorghe Hagi, Gică Popescu, Cristian Chivu, and Adrian Mutu.

Traditions

In many parts of the Romanian countryside, traditions are still practiced with enthusiasm. These are not just to attract tourists, either. Potters, woodcutters, icon painters, weavers, and embroiderers still work in their trade as their ancestors did. Romanian folk music is also famous far and wide. Some bands have become famous with a mixture of folk and pop music. There are, however, also many people who dislike this kind of music. This is unfortunate for them, since Romanian folk and pop music mixed together is usually played as loudly as possible.

◀ *Mr. and Mrs. Sas live in a village in the district of Maramureş, where their grandparents and great-grandparents also lived.*

Education

In recent years, there have been many changes in the education system. After the fall of the communist regime, new, previously ignored subjects were introduced and new textbooks were published.

There are many people who do not think that the current reforms are enough. According to them, major educational reforms are still needed.

▲ *The new school uniform*

Funding for education

People often complain that there is not enough money for education. The school buildings are frequently old and poorly maintained, the heating does not always work, and teachers do not get paid enough. Many teachers have second jobs or coach sports teams to make enough money to live. The problem of poor school facilities is not the only issue. Sometimes there are not even enough school buildings in a town or district.

In the communist era, all children belonged to a youth organization. Secondary schools were "Pioneers" and primary schools were "Falcons of the Fatherland." The Falcons wore orange blouses and a red tie as a symbol of communism.

The children then go to school in groups. Some groups go in the morning and others go in the afternoon. Staying at school over the lunch break is not common. Romanian children eat a large warm meal when they come home from school (or before they go).

◄ *This school is in the small western town of Sânnicolau-Mare.*

Despite reform efforts, the Romanian education system leaves much room for improvement. According to a report from 2007, Romanian public education does not prepare students well for life outside of school. The study shows that Romanian students do not do as well as their peers in other European countries.

▶ *Schoolbooks for sale in Obor Square in Bucharest*

▶ *School in the country, with recess finished*

School system

After nursery school, which lasts one to three years, all children go to primary school. They are seven when they go to primary school. This "general primary school" lasts eight years. It is compulsory, that is, required by law, and free for all Romanian children. Since 2008, school uniforms have also become compulsory at all state schools. This was originally eliminated after the revolution, but has now been reintroduced. Not everyone was happy about this reintroduction, but it is not likely that this law will be reversed any time soon.

Although attending primary school is required and free of charge, compulsory education is often skipped. In the country, farmers' children have to help on the farm. And not all of the Roma send their children to school either, since they do not usually have an education themselves.

◀ *Your student ID number and the name of your school is put on your sleeve.*

Though typical village schools have eight classes, this is not always the case. Sometimes there are only four classes. Sometimes the children have to go to a nearby, larger village that does have a school with eight classes. Public transportation is not always available and this means that they have to walk a number of miles in the morning and again in the evening if they want to pursue an education. That is not always possible, however. At school, children have to memorize basic subjects and there is little time for anything else. They do go on school trips regularly, though, to museums or monuments.

Soccer players in the city
One youth is a fan of Dinamo Bucharest and the other of Steaua. This doesn't mean they can't be best friends, though. After school, they play soccer between apartment buildings. The only thing they have to worry about is the ball landing between the cars. The ball is lost then and the game is over.

At the end of primary school, all children take what is called a proficiency exam in Romanian language and literature, mathematics, history, and geography. Students who want to study at a school for secondary education must pass their proficiency exams.

In 2007, making religious education compulsory came up for discussion. All recognized religions in Romania had asked for this. Religious education was offered at most schools, but a law that would make this mandatory was not passed. Students who do not want to be educated about religion, or who are not allowed to by their parents, have the opportunity in school to study a subject called religious *history*.

Icons in place of Ceauşescu

In the days of communism, a portrait of President Nicolae Ceauşescu hung in every classroom. After the revolution, those photographs were removed and replaced by icons, often a picture of Mary with the baby Jesus. In 2006, a teacher demanded that the icons and other religious symbols on the walls of schools be forbidden. The teacher claimed it was discrimination against non-believers and followers of non-Christian religions. For many months, both the supporters and opponents of icons in schools argued their case in the media. In the summer of 2007, the Romanian Court of Appeal ruled that religious symbols could only be hung up during religious education classes. This did not mean, however, that all icons were immediately removed from the walls.

Secondary school has four classes (five, if you are in an evening class). At the end of that schooling, students still have to take final exams. These final exams are made up of five tests: three written and two oral. The written and oral tests in Romanian language and literature are compulsory. Students can choose the other three subjects themselves.

Students who pass their final exams can study at one of the many universities, colleges, or vocational schools. First, however, they must take an entrance exam. For a number of subjects, such as medicine and information science, there are more candidates than places in the college program. Only the top students are admitted, and the others have to find another subject to study. To have a better chance of succeeding, future students take a year off to prepare for the entrance examination.

▶ *Students preparing for their study group*

A few years ago, higher education started to institute a bachelor and master degree system. This was adopted from the United States and is very similar to the system in Britain. It takes two or three years to study for a bachelor's degree. Beyond that, students will study a couple of years more for a master's degree. After that, a smaller number of students stay at the university to do research and gain a doctorate degree.

Romania not only has public state schools, but many private schools and universities as well. Students who do not succeed in getting into a state school may continue their studies at a private school. Private schools, unlike state schools, have tuition fees. Scholarships are available, but only the best students are able to obtain these.

Native language education

All students have the right to pursue their education at all levels in their native language. This right is, in practice, only for children who belong to a large minority group that does not speak Romanian. For example, children who are originally Hungarian can be taught in their own language from nursery school through the university. Recently, primary schools have also started to be taught in Romani, the language of the Roma. This is controversial because some fear that then Roma children will never learn to speak proper Romanian. Without knowing the national language well, finding a job after completing school will be much more difficult.

▶ *As a student, it's nice to earn some extra cash. Ioana helps her parents by working in their shop on the weekend.*

Cuisine

Romanians are hearty meat eaters. It's jokingly said that the tastiest vegetable is a piece of meat. Romanians do eat a lot of salads and potatoes, but cooked vegetables as a side dish are not popular.

Romanian cooking is similar to that of neighboring countries on the Balkan Peninsula, such as Bulgaria and Serbia. Romanian dishes have been influenced by Middle European, such as Hungarian, cuisine as well.

▲ *During the Cow Parade of 2005, painted cows could be seen everywhere in Bucharest.*

Markets

Supermarkets are becoming more and more popular, although Romanians still buy many food items at the traditional market. That is where farmers go to sell the produce they have grown. Many farmers, however, can no longer do this. Now it is necessary to produce food in surroundings that meet the health standards and strict regulations of the EU if they want to sell their products to the public.

▲ *The European Union no longer allows milk to be sold at the market or in the street.*

Many people in the country still live from what their small farms produce. They often keep a cow and a few chickens, and grow cabbages, tomatoes, cucumbers, and sweet peppers in their vegetable gardens.

▶ *A food shop*

Market in Craiova

This woman has been selling her herbs at the market in Craiova for years. It does not make her rich, but every little bit helps. It is also pleasant because other women from the village are there too. They enjoy talking together.

National Dishes

Romania has two national dishes. The favorite meat dish is *mici* or *mititei*, which literally means "little ones." These are spicy meat rolls with a little baking soda to lighten the color. They are tastiest when grilled and then eaten with mustard. In the winter, the favorite dish is *sarmale*, minced meat in cabbage leaves or grape leaves with sauerkraut and bacon, which should be eaten with *mămăligă* (corn grits). Corn grits used to be a staple food when bread was considered a luxury. Bread is now eaten with nearly every meal. Romanians enjoy eating their warm meals with a few chunks of bread.

Romanians often cook dishes that would not usually be found in other Western countries. The most traditional restaurants in Romania serve *ciorbă* de *burtă* (tripe soup).

▲ *Sarmale with mămăligă*

This soup is made from the stomach of cows. In many other countries, people would typically feed this part of the cow to dogs. Some people love tripe, while others would never consider eating it. Another delicacy in Romania that other countries may not be so fond of is calf's brains. In some Romanian restaurants that offer meat specialties, it is even possible to order a dish made from bear.

▶ *In Amsterdam, in the Netherlands, you can order tripe soup.*

Dracula

⚫ PREPARATE PE GRĂTAR
(HOOFDGERECHTEN VAN DE GRILL)

(toate preparatele pe grătar sunt servite cu cartofi prăjiți și salată)
(alle hoofdgerechten van de grill worden geserveerd met patates frites en salade)

1. **Mici**	
Mici (pittige Roemeense gehaktrolletjes)	€ 9.90
2. **Piept de pui**	
Kipfilet	€ 11.50
3. **Pulpe de pui**	
Kippenbouten	€ 11.50
4. **Ceafă de porc**	
Halskarbonade	€ 13.50
5. **Cotlet de porc**	
Varkenskotelet	€ 14.00
6. **Frigărui**	
Vleesspies	€ 14.90
7. **Mușchi de vită**	
Runderhaas	€ 16.10
8. **Grill mix**	
Mixed grill	€ 16.90

⚫ CIORBE
(SOEPEN)

1. **Ciorbă de legume**	
Groentesoep	€ 4.00
2. **Ciorbă de fasole cu afumătură**	
Bonensoep met gerookt vlees	€ 4.20
3. **Ciorbă de văcuță**	
Rundvleessoep	€ 4.20
4. **Ciorbă de burtă**	
Penssoep	€ 4.30

Restaurant Dracula

Roemeense traditionele keuken in Amsterdam!

Romanian snacks

What can you eat in Romania when you are walking through the city and suddenly feel hungry? How about a spicy roll with meat or cheese? *Covrigi*, a kind of large pretzel with sesame seeds, are delicious. Sometimes, though, you need strong jaw muscles to chew them. If you prefer something sweet, you can have apple tart or *gogoşi*, a kind of doughnut ball with raisins. In autumn, you can sometimes buy sweet chestnuts or bags of grilled corn on the cob. However, the fast food industry has arrived in Romania as well. So, if you don't like any of these options, you can satisfy your hunger with a hamburger. Or perhaps a more Romanian chicken kebab?

▲ *Romanians also love yogurt.*

Slaughtering and fasting

In Romania it is traditional to slaughter a pig a few days before Christmas. During the year, animals are fattened so that they can be placed upon the Christmas table at the end of the year. Because of the strict EU rules, the traditional slaughtering of the pig in the backyard will most likely end. The pigs have to be examined by food inspectors and made into chops and sausages in hygenic surroundings. This will make it difficult, if not impossible, to nibble on a piece of freshly roasted pig skin in a person's backyard. At Easter time, the Romanians traditionally eat lamb.

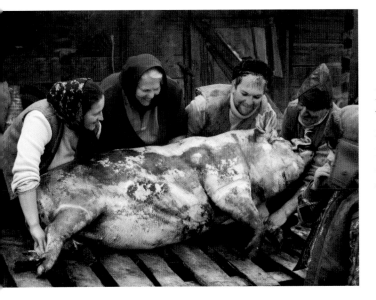

◄ *The pig slaughtered, everyone is looking forward to a delicious meal.*

Many Romanians of the Orthodox faith fast during various times of the year. This means that they are not allowed to eat certain kinds of food, especially meat, but also cheese and eggs. There are two periods of fasting for the Orthodox. The first is the seven weeks of fasting before Easter called the Great Fast, or Lent. The second is the forty days of the Christmas Fast. Exceptions are made for certain days during these periods. It is then allowed to eat fish and oil.

It is not possible to marry during the fasting periods. Marriages are always accompanied by huge festive meals that are spread out over several days.

▶ *A fish restaurant in the Olt valley*

Eating well in Romania means eating a lot. So, as a guest at the table, especially as a foreign guest, you will be encouraged to eat more than enough at a table already stocked with far more delicious food than you could possibly eat.

They never sting me....Well, almost never.

Natural honey

In the village of Şieu, in the far north, a bee-keeper lives. This beekeeper receives financial aid to make natural honey. The bees are fed on the acacia trees in the middle of unspoiled nature. There are no factories for miles and almost no traffic. However, when it comes time to sell his jars of honey on the European market, it is actually very difficult because of local regulations on food products.

Beverages

The Romanian national drink is *ţuică* (pronounced tsoejkeh) or *palincă* (twice distilled *ţuică*). It is usually made from plums. It can also be made from other fruit or pomace, the pulp that remains after pressing fruit. The European Union is planning to impose restrictions on the brewing of strong liquor, but people in the country will certainly not allow their tradition to be taken away without a fight.

In Roman times, wine-making already took place in the area that is now Romania. Serious wine-making was abandoned during the communist era. However, for a few years now, Romanian vineyards have been producing excellent wines again. The soil and the climate in Romania make for an excellent environment to grow grapes.

Romanians are also enthusiastic coffee drinkers. They sometimes take hours to drink a cup of coffee. The traditional Turkish coffee that is served throughout the Balkans is now declining in popularity compared to cappuccino, espresso, and other new drinks.

◄ *According to the label, this wine from Recaş gives you strength.*

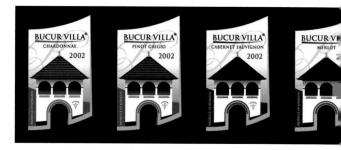

▲ *Romanian red wine from various types of grapes*

Recipe for Mititei

Ingredients
2 pounds of minced beef
pepper
cumin
1 teaspoon baking soda
salt
garlic
beef broth
1 teaspoon paprika (optional)

Mix a pinch of pepper, a dash of cumin, a teaspoon of baking soda, and salt (to taste) together with the two pounds of minced beef. If you like spicy food, mix in a teaspoon of paprika. Crush a generous amount of garlic cloves together with a dash of beef broth. Mix this into the minced beef and let it sit in the refrigerator for a couple of hours. If it is too dry, add a little more broth. Make small rolls from this mixture, about two inches long with a width of three-quarters of an inch. You can fry them, but it is better to grill them. Keep them moist by brushing them with the broth. Serve with mustard.

Economy

Romanians often say that they live in a rich country with poor inhabitants.

▲ *Hay is transported on an ox-cart.*

Romania has fertile soil, a pleasant climate, mineral deposits, the Danube River, the Black Sea, and a good location. It sits at the crossroads of trade routes between north and south. Yet, because of historical circumstances, such as falling under communist rule, Romanians have not always been able to enjoy all of this.

Late development

Romania is, above all, traditionally an agricultural country. Industry developed late here. Until the nineteenth century, 90 percent of the population lived in villages. Farmers usually worked for one person who owned the land or they had a small patch of land as their own. Most lived in great poverty.

From the end of the nineteenth century onward, industrial development began. In the period between the two world wars, Romania did make economic progress. After the borders had been expanded with Transylvania and Bessarabia, 80 percent of the population still lived in rural areas.

When the communists took power in Romania after World War II, all companies, factories, and shops were nationalized, or put under control of the state. The communist rulers wanted to industrialize the country quickly. They thought this was good for the economy, and also wanted to have support from laborers. There were, however, not many laborers in Romania. Traditional farming had to go and the farmers had to become farm laborers. This meant that they were forced to combine all their parcels of land together into a collective farm. If they did not have land to contribute to the collective farm, they were put to work on state farms.

▼ *The fields are ready to be sown, with the Carpathian Mountains in the background.*

▶ *If you don't own any land, your horses have to graze along the road.*

When the communist regime fell, Romania as a country was an economic disaster. Trucks, cars, aircraft, and oil tankers were built, but they were often poorly made. Companies had more people employed than western factories that produced the same items. Factories and the structure of businesses were out of date, and collective farming was both old-fashioned and inefficient.

◀ *The eight regions of ecconomic development (see page 14)*

Privatization and investment

The democratic government had the task from 1990 onward of reviving the economy. They decided to replace the communist economy with a market economy. In a communist economy, government leaders determine what and how much to produce. This is highly inefficient and results in shortages. In a market economy, individuals determine the prices of goods and how much of them to produce. With the transition to a market economy, private companies were allowed again. State-owned companies were sold to private firms or individuals. These were often foreign companies. Sadly, many old companies had to shut their doors or fire large numbers of people.

After several years of decline, Romania is starting to prosper again. For the most part, the economy has been growing since 2000. In 2004, economic growth was 8.2 percent. The possibility for a successful economy looks promising, especially because foreign companies are building new factories in Romania.

Foreign investment

On March 21, 2008, the Ford Motor Company made a major investment in Romania. The famous American firm bought Automobile Craiova, a car manufacturing plant built in 1976, from the Romanian government. Ford, the fourth-largest car maker in the world, planned to spend more than $900 million to upgrade the Craiova facility, which lies in southwestern Romania. At the time of the sale, the plant employed 3,900, but Ford expected to employ 7,000 people there eventually. The first vehicle off the assembly line, however, was neither a car nor a truck: it was the popular Transit Connect van, which can be outfitted for both cargo and passenger use.

▼ *Romania has a flourishing film industry. Some films have won international awards.*

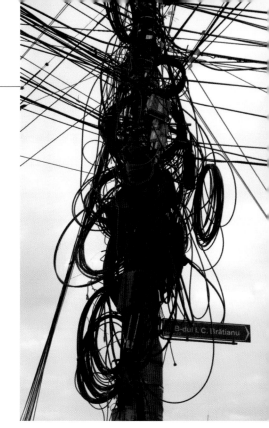

▶ *More Internet, more cables*

Germany and Italy are Romania's main trading partners, with France and Hungary also doing much business with Romanian firms.

Romania attracts many foreign investors because the country's employees are usually well trained. Moreover, the labor costs are low in comparison to Western Europe. This means companies that set up their businesses in Romania spend less money on employees than they would in other countries. For this reason, there are many contracting companies. As an example, textiles such as cotton are imported into Romania, fashioned into clothes, and then exported.

Aid

Romania receives a lot of money from the EU with which to develop and improve the infrastructure of the country. For example, the money goes toward building road systems and communications networks. An amount of 30 billion euros (about $40 billion) from the EU will be contributed from 2007 to 2012. About 60 percent of this will be set aside for the development of rural areas and agriculture.

◀ *When spring returns, you can buy fruit trees in the market.*

▼ *"I'm trying to earn a little extra! Won't you give me some coins for a song?"*

Accordionist

Mihai plays his accordion in the center of Bucharest. He keeps on smiling, but he is not really content. He receives a tiny pension (money from the government) and plays music to earn extra money.

Most Romanians earn very little money and there are hardly any unemployment benefits. For this reason, many workers have gone abroad, for example to Spain or Italy, in search of jobs that pay better than the ones at home. They have been doing this since 2001. Now that Romania is a member of the European Union, workers no longer need a visa to travel to other EU countries.

It is estimated that around 1.5 to 2 million Romanians work abroad. They send home much of the money that they earn. It is difficult for families, however, if the children have to stay behind with extended family or friends in Romania. Sometimes the children feel abandoned and miss their parents terribly. Yet, the Romanians make the decision to work abroad for higher pay in the hope of building a better future. The number of Romanian migrant workers is so great that there are often too few laborers to be found in Romania itself! This is especially true for the construction industry and in health care. For this reason, workers from neighboring countries, such as Moldova and Ukraine, and faraway countries such as Pakistan, Bangladesh, and China, come in large numbers to work in Romania.

▶ *Wooden kitchen utensils in a market in Craiova*

Home industry

Romania has an ancient tradition of folk art, folk dancing, and folk music. Home crafts and traditional handicrafts are also still popular. Pottery-making and carpentry are crafts that men traditionally do. Women traditionally do needle-work, knitting, crocheting, and weaving. Pottery, wooden objects, carpets, tablecloths, and small rugs are sold in the markets. Farmers also try to sell their crafts or agricultural products in places where Romanian and foreign tourists frequent. The money they earn from this is a welcome supplement to their regular income.

Larger Farmsteads

Around 20 percent of the Romanian population still lives in rural areas. With Romania's membership in the EU, it is widely expected that the conveniences of modern life will eventually reach the countryside. For now, however, a lot of traditional farming work is still done by hand on small plots of land. To become more economical, larger farmsteads will have to be established where work is done by tractors and combine harvesters. The Danube plain has the most fertile soil in Romania and is already used for agriculture. It is especially used to grow corn and wheat, although products such as soybeans (used as livestock feed) and rapeseed (for biofuel) are gaining more popularity.

Industry

Romania, a major oil producer historically, no longer has the reserves that it once had. New wells, however, have been drilled in the Black Sea. While the country still has an extensive petroleum industry, it now needs to import crude oil. The most important Romanian products are textiles and shoes, machines and motor vehicles, metal and metal products, and minerals and fuel. There is a large Renault factory in Piteşti, where the Dacia Logan is made. Most of Romanian trade is done with other EU countries, although Turkey is also an important trading partner.

▼*The Oasa reservoir in the mountains of Transylvania*

Tourism

Romania has great natural beauty, charming old cities, picturesque villages, the rugged Carpathian Mountains, and the sandy beaches of the Black Sea.

With all of this to offer, Romania has still never ranked high on the list of international tourist destinations.

Bran

Bran Castle towers high above the mountain pass that connects Transylvania to the south of Romania. At the end of the fourteenth century, the German community built an early version of this castle in the nearby town of Braşov. It has often been rebuilt, added onto, and strengthened through the centuries. It is also one of the biggest tourist attractions in Romania because of the beautiful mountainous terrain that surrounds it. It is presented as the castle of Dracula to attract tourists. Dracula, however, has no connection with this castle. Vlad the Impaler, who served as a model for the character of Dracula, spent only one night in this castle. Just in case, though, visitors are encouraged to hang a string of garlic around their necks since vampires are thought to hate garlic.

Growth of tourism

The Romanians see tourism as a growth market. Now that the country is a member of the EU, the number of foreign visitors will rise. At the same time, more and more Romanians take trips within their own country. New hotels and guest houses are being built everywhere. This will help tourism to become one of Romania's important growth industries.

Most tourists traditionally go to the sea and the mountains. Along the Black Sea, there is a whole string of resorts for those who love the sun and the sea. The Carpathians are a popular area for summer and winter vacations, for hiking and for skiing.

▼ The Selseş River

Romanians are lovers of nature themselves. On Sundays and public holidays, they gladly gather and eat dinner together on the green grass. Provided the weather is nice, of course, this makes for a lovely picnic. Romanians who live in the city, and can afford it, also build houses in the hills. Here, they escape the sounds and the stress of the city in their peaceful, beautiful, outdoor surroundings.

▶ *The Royal Palace Peleş in Sinaia with the nickname "Pearl of the Carpathians"*

Sinaia is a famous resort where the Royal Family of the United Kingdom used to stay. It has been given the nickname "Pearl of the Carpathians."

Tourists looking for sun and water visit the Black Sea. In recent years, however, as their country's economy improved, Romanian tourists have often vacationed in Bulgaria, Hungary, Greece, and more recently Tunisia.

The countryside

Romania's potential for expanding its tourist industry lies in small-scale tourism. Touring small towns and villages in the country is probably the most pleasant way to get to know the country. It is often possible and enjoyable to stay in a bed and breakfast house. Guest houses with only one or two rooms are also becoming more common in some parts of the country. Many tourists prefer to stay at these rather than in hotels. Most of the hotels have not been remodeled since the communist era.

Black Sea coast

Beach tourism is mostly located on the 45 miles of sandy beach running along the Black Sea. Romanians call it the Litoral. There are sixteen resorts along the seacoast. The resort Mamaia is the most famous. Young people prefer to get together in Costineşti. The resort 2 Mai is supposedly for those who love the sun and have an artistic side. Tourists from Romania and abroad visit the Litoral for a bath with the black mud from nearby lake Techirghiol. This is said to have healing effects for skin and bone diseases. Culture and history lovers can visit the remains of the Greek cities of Histria, Tomis, and Callatis. These were all established on the coast hundreds of years ago. Or, tourists can admire the Romanian mosaics and the archaeological museum of Constanţa.

▼ *Folk art is sold at the market in Craiova.*

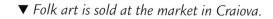

If tourists are traveling by car through Romania, Maramureş in the far north is a place that should not be overlooked. They can enjoy the scenery of the Iza Valley and admire the eighteenth-century churches and carved gates. Cutting through the Carpathians, they can go across the Prislop Pass (4,646 feet), which separates the regions of Maramureş and Bukovina, where frescos painted on the outside of churches hundreds of years ago retain their vibrant colors.

◀ *Frescos on the outside of a monastery in Sucevita*

▶ *Hunedoara is the biggest castle in Romania.*

The town of Sibiu is a beautiful example of Middle European architecture. There are charming, German-looking villages in the lovely rural surroundings of Mărginimea Sibiului. Many have fortified churches or church fortresses. These churches are from the early Middle Ages. People could be safe here from Tartars and other enemies looking to pillage and plunder.

▲ *Caru' cu bere menu*

Bucharest

Some parts of Bucharest are busy, dirty, and have run-down apartment buildings, but Bucharest itself is a dynamic and interesting city. "Ceauşescu's Palace," the Palace of the Parliament, can be visited if there is no congress or conference in session. Visitors can only see a small section of it, but that is enough to stand amazed at the sheer number of chandeliers, marble floors, and rooms (see page 10). The eighteenth-century Stavropoleos Church is also beautiful and worth visiting. Across the street is the Caru' cu bere (beer cellar), which dates back to 1879.

The open-air Village Museum is also fascinating. There tourists will see examples of traditional houses, windmills, and schools as they once could be found throughout the country.

Something for everyone

Romania likes to present itself as a country that has something to offer the visitor in every season. High temperatures often make the summer the least pleasant time to visit the country. That is, unless you have come to enjoy the intense sun of the Black Sea beaches or to visit the high mountains. Both spring and autumn are ideal for a tour through the Carpathians. However, the winter months are also worth a visit, especially for lovers of winter sports.

Adventurous tourists must not miss the impressive scenery of the Danube Delta. This can only be done by taking a boat trip through the maze of small waterways and little lakes with unique plant and animal life. Staying with local people, often originally Russian or Ukrainian, means waking up and falling asleep to the smell of freshly fried fish. Spoonbills, birds whose beaks look like a long spoon, and hundreds of other animals, are everywhere. With a little luck, a visitor many even see a colony of pelicans.

Romania was already well known for its mineral springs in Roman times. There are spas in many places now where people find relief from all kinds of ailments. The black mud found along the Black Sea is said to help in the treatment of rheumatism, a condition very much like arthritis that affects the joints.

▼ *Romania has many mineral springs, making mineral water a popular drink for cooling off.*

Nature

Romania's three most important geographical features are the Carpathians, the Danube River, and the Black Sea. For all, the scenery is varied and often unspoiled. For nature lovers, there is much to enjoy.

Mountains and valleys

The Carpathians are a mountain range that curves for a distance of 565 miles from north to west through the country. Four of the peaks of the Carpathians are higher than 8,000 feet. The highest is the Moldoveanu Summit (8,346 feet) in Făgăraş.

The lower sections of the Carpathians are called the sub-Carpathians. These are rolling hills that are often covered with dense woods. Mainly birch and sessile oak trees grow here. On the hillsides that are scattered with haystacks, sheep roam under the watchful eye of the shepherd. There are also many fruit trees in the hills, along with grapevines from which wines are produced.

◀ *A pelican colony in the Danube Delta*

Rivers and seas

The Danube River forms the largest river delta in Europe where it flows into the Black Sea. The Danube Delta has been on the World Heritage UNESCO list since 1991. Ninety percent of it lies in Romania and the other 10 percent in Ukraine. Although the delta is quite large, only 15,000 people live there. The only paved road in the Romanian part of the delta is in the little town of Sulina. The Danube Delta forms a maze of waterways and brooks, floating islands, and reedy lands where more than 1,200 species of plants grow, 300 species of birds nest, and 200 kinds of fish are to be found. Of these fish, the sturgeon is the most sought after for its caviar, a delicacy in most countries. There are also pelican colonies in the Danube Delta that are found hardly anywhere else in Europe.

The Romanian coast on the Black Sea is almost 124 miles long and, except for the Danube Delta, is made up of sandy beaches. The Black Sea is about 6,560 feet deep. Four other rivers flow into it, including the Dnieper, the Dniester, the Don, and the Kuban. The Black Sea has many fish down to a depth of 500 feet. Greater depths do not have much in the way of sea life, since little oxygen reaches the bottom.

▶ *A winter scene with church and river*

Forests

According to an old saying, Romanians are brothers of the forest. It is true that Romanians love their forests and sing about their beauty in folk songs and traditional poetry. The country used to be almost completely covered in forests. Now, they cover only about a quarter of the land. The woods and forests were good hiding places for people who sought shelter from invaders or bandits. Or, the bandits themselves sometimes hid in the woods. Sadly, illegal deforestation takes place since money can be made from selling wood. This is not good for the environment and increases the risk of erosion and flooding. In 2003, the government began a program for reforestation. For the time being, however, there is not enough money to run this program effectively.

National Parks

Romania has eleven national parks that are accessible only to hikers. The total area is 1,532 square miles. The country's oldest is the Tetezat Park, which became a national park in 1935. In its 208 square miles, 900 species of plant life grow. In the Carpathians, bears are so bold that they go into the villages in search of food. People have been injured who could not get out of their way quickly enough. Bears are hunted on a minor scale. Other rare animals, however, can feel safe in these national parks. Such animals include the wisent, the European bison, which is a relative of the North American bison and the heaviest land animal in Europe.

Caves

Hundreds of caves are hidden in the mountainsides of the Carpathians. One of the most famous is Bear Cave. The cave was given this name because hundreds of skeletons of cave bears, which became extinct 15,000 years ago, were found there. This cave was discovered in 1975, is 4,921 feet long, and full of stalagmites, deposits of calcium carbonate that form upward from the floor of the cave, and stalactites, deposits of calcium carbonate hanging from the roof of a cave.

▶ *The pollution of the town Copşa Mică can be seen in these computer enhanced aerial photos. Carbon black for car tires was produced here.*

Environment

The environment was completely ignored during the communist era. The only thing that mattered was producing as much as possible. It did not matter if black clouds of smoke billowed out of factories. In 1990, Copşa Mică became famous as the "filthiest town in Europe." The factories that polluted the most have now been closed. As a member of the European Union, Romania must keep to the strict environmental rules that the EU has set up. The environmental awareness of the Romanian people is increasing, but a truly "green" way of thinking has not yet been developed. Repairing the damage done to the environment by the communists will continue well into the future.

▶ *In this aerial photograph of Copşa Mică in 2004, the polluted area has decreased, but the environment is still not fully cleaned up.*

Glossary

Communism A political system based on the principles of government control of property and public speech.

Dacia Conquered by the ancient Romans, this large territory north of the Danube and west of the Dniester rivers covered what are now the countries of Romania and Moldova.

Habsburg Empire The lands, including much of modern-day Romania, that were under the control of the Austrian royal family from the late Middle Ages to the twentieth century.

Moldavia A historic principality that covers roughly the eastern half of Romania.

Ottoman Empire A great Muslim power, based in Turkey, that conquered and ruled much of Europe for centuries until 1918.

Transylvania A territory of west-central Romania that has long been home to many ethnic Hungarians.

Wallachia A historic principality that covers most of the southern half of Romania.

Index

Websites

https://www.cia.gov/library/publications/the-world-factbook/geos/ro.html
www.romaniatourism.com
www.lonelyplanet.com/romania
http://www.worldstatesmen.org/Romania.htm
http://romania.net/